ENGLISH VERSION by STAN ATAMANCHUK

TAO TE CHING

English Version
by Stan Atamanchuk.

Lao-tzu's the ancient Chinese Zen Master left only his book: TAO TE CHING, Chinese, meaning "the way" or Book of the Way. TAO is defined as the flow of Nature. When you see clouds float in the sky you are seeing the way of the TAO ...ever changing, ever flowing. At a deep level we are a field of waves. The TAO, the basic, eternal principle of the universe that transcends reality and is the source of being, non-being, and change. The source and principle of the cosmic order; the constant flow of life force in unceasing change.

ENGLISH VERSION by STAN ATAMANCHUK

TAO TE CHING translation

I would like to thank...

Lao-tzu for having the courage to speak the truth,
I have a deep respect for his wisdom.

1.

The TAO that can be spoken is not the forever TAO.

The name of the TAO uttered is not the forever TAO.

That which is unnamable is real forever.

Origins start with names.

When you become desire-less you will realize the mystery.

When you are trapped by desire you see only the physical side of things,

the manifestations.

Manifestations and this mystery arise from the same center which is nothingness.

Nothingness within nothingness, the pathway to understanding all.

2.

When you call something beautiful, then by course of action you must call other things ugly.

When you assume one thing is good, then other things appear bad.

In order to have being ...first you must have non-being.

They support each other as in a dance.

One moves the other into the light of experience.

Easy and difficult are swirling together in this dance.

So are short and long.

High and Low caress each other.

Before and After are each a shadow of one another.

To be a Master you act without doing.

You teach without saying a single word.

A Master allows things to Rise and Fall.

This is the way of the TAO.

Actions have no real end.

They just are.

Approaching all events with no expectations.

When your work is done you forget it.

That is why it is forever

3.

If you make one man great then others become powerless.

Stealing arises from over valuing of physical things.

A Master leads by clearing her mind.

A Master leads by filling his core.

Ambition should be weakened.

Resolve is your strength.
Build it ...letting nothing distract you.

People who think they know everything should be avoided.

People who think they know everything are truly confused.

Practice not doing and everything will fall into place.

<u>4.</u>

The TAO is like the flame of a candle that can light millions of other candles and is never diminished.

The TAO is like the gap between your thoughts....filled with endless possibilities.

You do not see the TAO but it is always here and always has been.

The TAO transcends even your concept of a creator.

It is like the plastic creation was molded from.

5.

In the TAO there is no idea of good or evil.

It just is.

A Master strives to stay in the middle.

She judges not......welcoming both Sinners and Saints.

The TAO is like your lungs:

Empty yet life springs from it.

Anything is possible as a result of its movement.

The more you breathe the more you live. When you speak of your lungs can you know why you take your next breath?

Hence the TAO.

The power is between the breaths.

Look to the center.

Be advised you cannot grasp the center......it is the wisp of the wind......the breath of the TAO.

<u>6.</u>

The TAO is like a great father: in his loins issues forth infinite realms.

The TAO is always with you and can be used anyway. It is your choice.

7.

The TAO is forever.

Why forever?

It will never die because it was never born.

Being here to help all things it is desire-less. It is in all things. It has no intentions for itself. The TAO just is.

A Master is at the front because he stays behind.

She is not attached.

He is flexible.

A Master is one with all things.

Letting go, the Master Flows in their TAO.

In letting go perfect fulfillment is attained.

<u>8.</u>

The ultimate way is like air, which gives life to all things without effort. It is everywhere. Therefore it is like the TAO.

Live as close to the earth as you can.

Think of things in simple ways.

Strive for fairness and be generous.

Resist the need to control.

Do what you enjoy.

When you are with your loved ones practice

"being here now".

Be you.

Don't compare or compete.

This will bring you respect.

9.

Your bowl will only hold so much.

Learn to know the balance.

Strive to let it be.

Chasing after money and security will only create stress inside your being.

Unclench your hand and it will be freely given to you.

If all you do is worry about people's approval then you are their slave.

When you have finished your work, relax.

A Master finds serenity's path by relaxing.

10.

A persons mind naturally wanders.

If we could only become as a newborn child.

Seeing the light in the day as its oneness....untouched by adult judgments.

Can you lead and not impose your own personal will?

Strive to deal with only the most vital matters and let events take their natural course.
Can you look at even your own mind from a distance...thereby understanding all things?

When you start something support it. You don't have to own anything. Do you really own anything?

When you die where does it go? With you?
I think not.

Take your actions with no expectations.

When you do you will be open to anything that happens and therein not be disappointed.

A child never knows what is going to happen next.

They see all things with wonderment, seemingly grateful for all outcomes.

Recapture that. It is in you.

Can you lead and not try to control?

It appears one must surrender.

This is the virtue of all virtues.

11.

All things are connected.

Like a wheel with spokes.

The spokes turn around the center hole. Everything turns around emptiness.

The wagon of life moves around an empty center.

A clay pot is shaped around the emptiness that holds things.

A house has walls...but you live in the emptiness between them.

We work with things but it is the non-being of our thoughts that we really use.

Things are not thoughts.

Thoughts are not things.

Mental note:

All things start as thoughts,

which is nothing.

12.

When you see color what are you really seeing?

When you hear a sound what are you hearing?

When you taste a flavor? What do you taste?

In your mind when you have a thought...of what is it made?

In your heart, your longings, desires, and dreams...from whence do they come?

The Master knows all things in the world are a reflection of his inner reflection.

She allows things to rise and fall.

His heart is open like the sky full of Sun, Moon and Stars.

13.

Why do you consider yourself either a success or failure?
Hope and Fear are two parts of the same trap.

The best you can do is feeling inside their Optimum Divine Destiny. When you feel it... you will feel balanced like both your feet are planted firmly on the ground. Unshakable, you will "Know".

What do I mean when I say Hope and Fear are part of the same trap? When you have hope or fear in both cases you are thinking of your identity you have created for yourself.

You are more than that.

You are more than a woman.
You are more than a man.
You are more than a mother.

You are more than a father.
You are more than a brother.
You are more than a sister.

You are more than a daughter.
You are more than a son.
You are more than a wife.
You are more than a husband.
You are more than you think you are.

If this is so, then why bother worrying about your
illusion?
Your identity.

It can all be gone in a twinkle of an eye.

So what is there to hope for and what is there to fear?

If you see the world as your self then you will not fear
it.

Trust in the fact that "This moment is as it should be."

It always has been...it always will be.

Then you can relax.

Breathe.

Love all things as yourself.

Care for all things as yourself.

Be the light of the Star you are.

14.

Look for it and you can't see it.

Listen for it and it can't be heard.

Reach for it and it can't be touched.

Above is not brightness.

Below is not dark.

Untraceable it returns to nothingness.

Forms of all forms contained therein.

Images of all are therein.

It is subtle, transcending all known things.

Try to find its beginning.

Try to find its end.

You can't meet it but you are it.

Relax be you and you will know it.

When you think of yourself, start in the essence of nothingness.

The essence of wisdom.

15.

The Masters of the past were deep and shallow.

You would never have known if others did not draw attention to them.

Their wisdom vibrates now in your being.

In your memory their words now ring.

Words are hollow scratches written on the image of mankind. You only know what you see... there is much unseen.

As a Master she is careful like walking over slippery ice. As a Master he is alert like a Warrior King.

As a guest a Master approaches all things.

Flowing in his path, like melting snow finding the easiest way. Shapes of a Master can change like carving a block of wood. Open like a valley.

The most pure of all waters.

Can you wait? The silt will settle then the waters are clear. Can you wait?

Can you sit still and let the right action arise by itself?

The Master doesn't look for anything.

She is not seeking.

He is not expecting.

She is here now and welcomes all things into her path.

16.

Clear your mind.

Ring the gong.

Find the gap between your thoughts.

May your heart be at peace?

Beings naturally are in turmoil, wait for their return.

We all return to the common core of peace and serenity.

Knowing the source keeps you safe in the strong waves of change.

Remember where you come from and you will accept all others.

Seek virtues as a King does for his Kingdom.

Be kindhearted as a Queen to her subjects.

When you are balanced in your own TAO you can flow through whatever wave life sends you.

When death does come, you are ready.

17.

Find a Master if you can...for those she governs hardly knows she exists.

Under that leaders are loved.

Next some are feared.

Last those that are despised.

If you see the people as being untrustworthy, then they will be.

The Master acts with little fanfare.

The people say "Look how we did this!"

<u>18.</u>

Forget the TAO, goodness and piety arise.
Patriotism arises from the rubble of chaos.

<u>19.</u>

Don't try to be holy.

Just be.

Don't try to be wise.

Just be.

Don't try to be moral

Just be.

Don't try to be just.

Just be.

Thieves cannot survive where there is no value.

Stay in the center of things.

The TAO makes its own course.

Just watch.

<u>20.</u>

Do you feel you think too much sometimes?

Stop thinking...your problems vanish!

Why do you feel you have to decide everything?

No or Yes.

Does it really matter?

Does it really matter if you win or lose?

Just because "they" think it's of value...is it?

If "they" don't want it does that mean you can't desire
it?

Think about it....it's funny.

Do you need to care like others do?

When "they" get excited...do you have to?

Is there anything wrong with being blank?

Expression-less?

Where is your innocence?

Is it not found in not reacting?

Other people feel they must own.

Do they really?

Is there anything wrong with drifting like the wind?

Are you afraid to empty your mind?

Does the silence and stillness of the cave scare you?

Bright...... dark.....sharp....dull....does it matter?

Just because "they" have a purpose....do you have to?

Is there anything wrong with drifting like a wave on
the ocean?

Like dust in the breeze?

Do "they" think you are different?

Drink from the cup of the TAO.

Be You.

21.

The radiance of a Master flows from the TAO.
This is why you ponder it.

Do not grasp after the TAO.
Do not push it away.
Flowing non-clinging is the way.
Your ideas are only that.
Let them go.
If they are to be they will.

You say you cannot see the TAO.
Then how can it be radiant?
Let it be.

Your ideas of time and space are imagined.
Beyond not and is.
The TAO.
Prove it you say?
Look inside yourself.
You will see nothing.
The TAO.

22.

If you seek wholeness, then accept the fact you are partial.

Embrace your crookedness to become straight.

Observe your emptiness ...you will be full again.

You cannot be reborn without dying.

To receive everything unclench your hand ....give it up.

Others notice how a Master walks.

Where she steps ...how she moves.

He flows in his TAO.

Only natural.

No struggle.

There is a glow about him.

She beams like a lighthouse.

People trust a Master because they can clearly see he has nothing to prove.

Not trying to impress she just does her works.

He is transparent.

She reflects like a mirror.

It's easy to see yourself in a Master.

Because he is not trying to win...but to learn...it is easy to lead the way.

Everything she does succeeds.

Knowing that seeking is the way.

The TAO.

When you find your way...your TAO....your expectations cease.

Then you can be you.

Embrace yourself.

23.

Express yourself like the forces of nature.

Wind, rain, clouds, sun.

There is a time for everything.

A season for all the parts of you.

Your life has stages as you grow.

Storms only last a short while.

Express yourself ....then be calm as the river.

Rise, fall.

Remember there is a part of you that always shines like
the sun...even when you sleep.

Open yourself to the TAO.

Your stress is only imagined.

A river just flows.

Flow.

You never hear a river cry for loss.

It knows its nature...its TAO is to rise and fall.

Accept this about yourself.

Even this moment we are whirling though uncharted space.

The emptiness of the universe.

We always have.

Trust this way....the TAO.

Trust your natural response.

Everything falls into place.

The acorn will find the ground.

Hence the Oak.

24.

The flow continues.

Stand firm well connected to the earth.

Relax and you will find your proper place.

Do not try to shine. Doing so will only dim your brightness.

Realize that without any effort of your own you are a Star-seed.

It is the nature of a Star-seed to shine.

Allow yourself to drift on your path.

Let go and flow in your TAO.

When you strive for power over others you lose the ability to empower yourself.

Do not cling to your work.

Things that endure are not forced.

Spend each moment looking for your TAO, your flow.

Do whatever it takes to stay in that flow and then let go.

25.

In the nothingness before creation there is perfection.

Peaceful, non-moving, empty.

No change, by itself it is whole, endless, always there.

This nothingness is the hole from which we spring giving birth to the universe.

Not knowing what to call this nothingness which is nameless, I simply call it the TAO.

It flows through all you observe and things you cannot observe. It is the source and the force. The channel on which all things can been seen.

The TAO, the universe, earth and man. All linked and flowing together, one to the other, connected like a huge web. The TAO the foundation of all.

Like the clay God formed man from is the TAO.

<u>26.</u>

Heavy and light are deeply connected by a root.

How do you see the flower grow?

The source is unmovable.

Thus a Master Travels without moving.

The views moving by her.

Like a flower unfolding enjoys the dance of newness.

No need to float here and there.

Hold on to your root not being blown to and fro.

Be calm and unfold naturally not being restless and
losing touch with who you are.

27.

A Master does not feel their life running down but instead reaching a deeper level.

A wise traveler has no fixed plans and is not anxious about arriving.

Therein you learn to flow, letting go of the tightness from within.

A good artistic writer paints the picture with words letting his intuition flow out expressing, creating.

A good scientist views what is and has no concepts of what it should be.

A Master is here for all and does not turn away anyone.

In all situations he finds the way. With least effort. Hardly a ripple is made. Yet it moves all about him.

She knows all things are based in light.

The good man teaches the bad man.

The bad man gives the good man a reason to teach.

If you don't get this you will get lost, makes no difference how smart you think you are.

It is the secret of secrets. A closed mind stays shallow.

28.

Being male you need to try to understand the female.

Being female you need to try to understand the male.

Embrace every gender into your arms.

If you embrace and accept people then the TAO will be with you in your innocence.

Innocence is the allowing things to be as they are part of you.

No matter what color, try to understand it.

Inside you are all colors.

Colors are only wave patterns.

Your pattern can be seen by the world.

Tune your pattern to the TAO, everything is possible.

Know your character, yet accept all characters.

Accept this planet as it is.

When you do you will be seen as a light for all to see, as your primal seed is Star-seed.

Star-seed as everything is made from the TAO.

Practice delayed reaction for then you have a chance to consider your next movement.

When you feel inside your TAO, then move.

Everything, even your slightest intentions are made from the TAO.

This is what a Master stays close to, the TAO.

If your moments are sometimes filled with great pain, then you can learn as mothers know that sometimes great joy can be born after great pain.

Search for the joy at the end of your pain.

It is there waiting to live.

You can be there when it comes with a smile.

Greet that joy that is born with love.

29.

Improving the world?

I'm not sure it can be done.

Since we all live in our own world, can we expect for us to agree?

If you notice someone is on the same vibe you are then that is good.

Don't expect everybody to be.

Just don't expect, instead experience what is.

If you can have no expectations then you can find peace.

So accept the world as being sacred.

Not needing improvement.

Instead strive not to improve the world, but yourself.

Tamper with the world and lose it.

Treat it as an object and you will ruin it.

There is a time for being #1.

There is a time to be the last one.

A time to lunge forward.

A time to sit effortlessly.

A time to overflow with energy.

A time to recharge.

A time to be in the womb of safety.

A time to be in the flowing world of change.

As a Master, she sees things as they are, accepting
without control.

Sitting at the center of the circle, she watches things go
in their own flow, their own TAO

Enjoying the process.

30.

If you follow the TAO in governing people you don't try to force things, or defeat foes with force.

Even violence with best intentions only causes more violence, sometimes creating an endless loop of karma. If you don't know the meaning of karma I suggest you get to know it, something that has been with you all your life, having effects on you even this moment.

A Master observes the TAO of the universe. Knowing his TAO flows in that TAO, he just does his work and forgets it.
Flowing against the current of the TAO is possible, but only makes life more difficult. You can get somewhere, but it takes much more energy.

Don't worry about what others think or say, they will never understand your TAO, only you can.

Your flow is your flow, so flow in it.
Be content. You can inspire others if you have the courage to follow your TAO. They will notice it. Accept yourself and your TAO, others will too.

31.

Weapons can only destroy, giving the wave of fear a reason to continue, avoid it at all cost. Use them only as a last resort, with restraint.

Peace is the highest you can seek, shatter the peace, and how can you feel the flow?

Your foes are not demons but humans like yourself.

Do not wish them personal harm, nor celebrate when you defeat them.

Never delight in the falling of another.

There are times in this life when we must enter the battle, do so as if attending a funeral, with great loving compassion.

32.

Look for the TAO, you won't find it.

The TAO is smaller than you can imagine yet contains all of the universes.

If leaders could stay centered in the TAO then there would be peace.

The TAO is written in their hearts.

The problem is people don't know when to stop, knowing when to stop is the key.

Lay low, you will be in your TAO like a river lays low and finds the ocean.

33.

Knowing everybody on the planet will only give you
information.

Wisdom springs from knowing yourself.

Strength is in numbers, still they are only people.

Real power comes from within.

Master yourself.

If you are grateful for what you have,

then you are truly rich.

You live in the center.

Looking from the center, if you do not fear death, you
can endure.

34.

The TAO is like the air, in everything, around everything.

It gives everything life yet it did not begin it.

It's work is manifesting creation, yet it is not the author.

The TAO is in all worlds, yet is not attached to any of them.

Being behind the scenes, the TAO, the flow.

All things return to it, not a being, a process.

Like a path, not just a path.

The TAO will always find the best way.

Like a river finding it's bed.

Your body gives you signals, so find your TAO.

Many people stay so distracted, stop, touch, look, listen, taste, smell, behold the TAO.

With no boasting it is truly great.

<u>35.</u>

When you are centered in the TAO you can go where you wish without danger.

As a master universal peace will find you even in the midst of great pain, she bares the burden, since peace lives in her heart.

People are thrilled by the sound of music, or the smell of cooked food, yet the TAO seems boring to them so they yawn.

Look and you will not see it, reach out your hand and you will not touch it, use it everlasting.

<u>36.</u>

Before you can change the size of anything, you must first allow it to be what it is.

Before you can get rid of something, first it must grow.

Before you take, it must be given.

This is part of the mystery of how things are.

Soft overtakes hard, slow overcomes fast.

Let your work be a mystery, just show the results.

A Master is not affected by other's poison, no matter what she stays in love.

37.

Think about it, the TAO never takes any actions yet by it all actions happen.

The TAO is about natural movements like the gathering of sand into dunes on the beaches. If only leaders could be centered in the TAO then problems

would naturally gather a solution over time. This seems like fantasy, yet have you seen a beach lately? The dunes were there before either one of us and

will be there after we leave. They just move naturally. It is part of their TAO to change and move. So it is with you. You would be happier with your

everyday life, free of desire. Does a dune desire to be a man or woman? We gaze at them and wonder. If only we could just accept ourselves and be

who we are like the dune, in harmony with it's flow, it's TAO.

Does the sand in the dune have desire? No.
Could be that is why it is at peace.

People have asked me how can you live without
expectations or desires.

It's really pretty simple if you can just be here now.

Most desires reach into the future or reach back to try
to fix the past.

Just don't do that. Be here now, like the new bud on
the rose bush at the side of your house. Take time to
stop and smell it. It is a simple pleasure, one

of the types that arises naturally, if you can be here
now. Not back in the past or way in the future. Focus
your mind like a laser.

38.

A Master knows she is powerful. She can feel it inside, she does it without effort.

The frustrated man strives for power, he never gets enough.

The Master knows at her core is nothing, so she does nothing, leaving nothing undone.

The frustrated woman is always thinking of new things to do, never satisfied, yet never gets anything done.

The kind woman does good works, yet there is always more healing needed.

The just woman does one thing, leaving many things yet to do.

A moral person will take whatever action is needed to follow the truth with dignity, even willing to give all for it.

Lose your TAO and find good things.

When you lose good things you will become moral.

Rituals arise when you lose morals.

The outer shell of knowing is action.

You cannot escape chaos so don't even try.

A Master looks to the core, the deepness, not the outer surface.

The fruit is what a Master looks for, the flower is just a distraction.

Her will does nothing because there is none.

A Master lives in what is and lets all imagined illusions float by, like clouds in the sky.

39.

When you are in harmony with the TAO your whole world will be balanced. You will see the sky as flowing in its TAO, the plants, the animals, all

flowing in their true paths. It is like a great song played from a timeless drum. The beat is right, the song is heartfelt from deep within your being.

When man gets in the way of the TAO the sky becomes black, the waters polluted, the ground like a sore, the animals disappear.

A master views all the parts and feels a wholeness.

He takes actions that keep him humble.

Some will laugh saying how can she do this ?

Yet he knows how to harness his emotions.

She knows that being like a stone is just as important as being like a jewel.

What is a jewel ?

Only a stone that has been overvalued.

40.

Finding it's way home is the way of the TAO.

When you relax this is what will happen.

You will go home.

Not forcing things to please others is the way of the TAO. Don't struggle, remember you don't have to do anything, especially please others. When you find someone is trying to change you, just walk away.

All things come from the nothingness, then the cycle begins. Like a ripple on the ocean creating a new beginning. Do not be afraid of starting over.

<u>41.</u>

A man trying to evolve embraces the TAO.

Some men half believe the TAO.

Some think it's foolish to study the TAO.

Maybe because the TAO is so incredible it seems not to be true.

42.

The TAO, the nothingness, is the genesis of one,
one vibrates with intention, intelligence, behold two,
two seeks to create three.

Without 3 there is not structure. With 3 anything can
manifest and multiply.

All manifest things carry the yin...the female and the
yang...the male.

When they meet in harmony it is total bliss.

The average person detests solitude, the master uses it
as a great tool.

The master desires to be one with the entire universe,
aloneness does not exist for him.

43.

Look at a woman; she can subdue any man with her charms. Look at the water it can wear down any rock. Feel the air so gentle on your face, yet it can

blow you off the mountain top. This is what is meant by the softest things overcoming the hardest things. This is why it is so important to relax in all

you do. In that gentle relaxation you will find your real power.

Nothingness is in all things. Think about it. Everything springs from nothing, the unknown. Even now you don't know what I will write next, neither

do I. Each action begins with non-action. Start there.

Non-action.

Teaching without words, performing without actions, this is the way of the Master.

44.

Your impeccable word or being well known: which matters most?

A happy life or money: which do you value?

What can destroy you? Success or Failure?

If you allow others to control your pleasure then you will never have it.

Never let others control your self esteem.

If you think money will bring you happiness then you will never really understand happiness.

The best you can do is be happy with what you have and be grateful for the way things are.

When you realize the whole world belongs to you, then you will be happy, there is not a thing lacking.

45.

Perfection? How can you decide when it seems imperfect?

When each thing is what it is, it is perfect.

Fullness? How can you decide when it seems empty?

What seems empty can be full.

Things that are straight can seem crooked.

Wisdom can seem foolish.

Artful things can appear artless.

The challenge of a Master is to just relax and allow life to happen.

Let the waves of life come to you, and then ride them.

The key is being relaxed.

You can shape this dream as it comes to you.

Strive to step back and let the TAO just be.

Not trying to control it, if you do, your effort is truly wasted.

46.

If you spend your time making productive things then you are in harmony with your TAO.

If you spend time trying to think of ways to defend yourself then you are going counter to your TAO.

Fear is an illusion, preparing to defend yourself causes fear and the cycle never ends.

To have an enemy is very stressful.

If you are the lucky one who can see through fear, past its illusion, then you will have peace and be safe.

This all might sound too simple, yet wisdom sounds like folly to a fool.

47.

You can sit right where you are and love the whole world.

You can feel everything, for you are a part of everything.

The TAO is right before your eyes.

The more you think the less you understand.

The TAO is felt.

A Master can be there without going, can see without looking.

A Master relaxes and does anything.

48.

When you go seeking wisdom that is the one thing you want to add to yourself, keep it, seek it daily.

When you go seeking the TAO you let go of things, try to let go more everyday.

Unclench your fist.

You will find that when you truly are relaxed and trust the process of the TAO in your life you will not feel the desire to force things.

It will appear that you are doing nothing, yet everything is done.

When you truly relax in your TAO, not someone else's, but yours, it will make everything come to you, like a cosmic magnet.

This is because what is truly part of your path is seeking you as much as you are seeking it.

It is part of your destiny.

The key is relaxing.

When I say "relax", I do not mean non-action but relax while your are taking the action.

A Master lets things go where they will and not interfering.

A Master is relaxed.

People ponder how a Master does all he does because he appears so relaxed.

49.

A Master has no mind of his own; he understands that all thoughts are connected to the universe.

He understands that his thoughts are part of the whole mind process.

It's easy to be good to people who are good, a Master is good to those who aren't good because he knows the process is good.

It's easy to trust people who can be trusted; a Master trusts those who can't be trusted because he trusts the process.

A Master seems strange to most people, like his mind is empty, he just sits and waits, then reacts.

A Masters mind is childlike, open to new experiences, eager to learn.

Yet he lets go of things not good for his path.

<u>50.</u>

A Master accepts death as part of his path.

He lets go and doesn't resist.

His mind is clear, knowing that all things rise and fall, including him.

He doesn't think much because his actions come from his inner core, thinking is not needed.

He puts his all into every moment, holding on to nothing, letting go of things so they can flow their own way.

Like a man ready for sleep, a Master is ready for death, after having a very good day.

51.

Everything that exists springs from the TAO.

At a deep level everything honors the TAO.

The TAO is like a great mother that takes care of you,
keeping you on your way, whatever way you choose.

The TAO creates yet does not own.

With no expectations the TAO acts.

Letting things go the way they will, that is the way of
the TAO.

This is what is known as going with the flow.

52.

Trace things back to their beginnings and there you will find the TAO.

The TAO is like the plastic the creator force used to make everything.

You want to feel pain? Let me tell you how...judge things...then desire things.... when you don't receive your desires......that is where the pain is.

The only way to stop this pain is to control your mind, which is like a team of wild horses running here and there. Reins must be held tight, do not let

your emotions rule, or let your senses lead, this is the only way to peace.

Refocus your attention on positive actions because this dream we all live in rewards actions.

You can see clearly in darkness if you know that there really is no darkness.

Nothingness is the beginning of all creations, from nothing you were born, look at you now.

Knowing when to yield makes you strong.

Inside, you are pure light, it is from the source, made from the TAO, and it is linked to eternity.

Go there often.

53.

Finding your TAO, your path, is easy, but most people prefer going off the path.

It appears that when you are on your path you are naturally relaxed and centered.

When you go off your TAO, your path, you will feel unbalanced.

I wonder if this is why people like to go off their natural path.

Because when you do, it apparently gives one a feeling of being off balance,

the same way a drunk person feels the thrill from being off balance when drunk.

It appears that this feeling of being off balance or drunk for a short while is thrilling to some. Being drunk or off balance makes a person forget who

they are. This is sad.

All it does is make your path harder and it slows you down.

Why would you want to be off balance and forget who you are?

I say stay balanced on your path, your TAO.

Avoid anything that would make you feel off balance.

Only you can feel your TAO.

Feel your internal signals.

Do not compare your TAO, your path, to others.

Give and takes are natural actions.

We are all here to grow so it is natural to gain; there is nothing evil with gain.

Is it evil for a tree to grow, or gain? No, it's natural.

Yet that same tree gives back, in the form of fruits from its branches, even its leaves fall to feed the ground it grew from below it.

This is giving back, the tree is paying it forward, it's natural.

In your business you gain but do you give back?

Set up a way for yourself to give.

To pay it forward.

54.

Plant yourself in the TAO and you will grow.

Just look at a tree.

It's planted in the TAO.

Think about a tree, it doesn't really try to hide anything; it's all out there for you to see.

So if you are planted in the TAO you will become a genuine person, straightforward, with nothing to hide, like the tree, all its fruits hang from its limbs.

55.

A master sees the eternal moment with her childlike eyes.

His grip is strong and never tires.

Her gaze is long, why should she blink?

His voice is strong, primal, and pure.

A master swims in the stream of the eternal moment.

Diving in playful and childlike, never drowning in the worries of others.

What is worry?

When you are in your TAO worry does not exist.

56.

You don't have to know to talk.
Words will flow to you when you are in your TAO.

Thinking is not needed,
like a natural dance you will know the right words.

Bring in your senses,
touch your inner power,
let your emotions settle.
You will find the real you.

Connect in your TAO,
you will not feel judgment.
Judgments are imagined.
Go between your thoughts.
Stop images of judgment.

The TAO is ever changing,
so are you.
How can you judge something that is always changing?

<u>57.</u>

Processes do not rule people, be it paper or virtual.

A persons TAO is for them only, so if you are a ruler, do not try to be to detailed in setting someone's direction or TAO.

Let your workers set their own TAO.

What is your TAO?

Only you know.

So do not decide your neighbors TAO.

Find yours and flow in it and help your neighbors find theirs.

This is what is meant by take no action, relax in the flow of your TAO.

You must put one foot in front of the other but always know that the ground before you is your TAO.

Your TAO is simple. So is everyone's.

Simple.

<u>58.</u>

Don't mettle in peoples business, which only makes
them disappointed.

Misery and happiness are in a dance of balance, one is
always near the other.

A Master is flexible, she moves with the flow, sensitive
of hers and everyone's TAO.

No one is hurt.

She is like a Star in the deep night sky, even though
she could, she shines but does not try to bewilder with
spectacular display.

<u>59.</u>

The TAO is balanced, a perfect flow.

A Master uses moderation when it comes to her actions.

He makes sure his actions do not create bad karma, which sends things out of balance.

She does what is best for all concerned including herself.

When you use moderation you will stay in your TAO.

A Master brings under control; conquers desires.

Have no intentions of limits.

Let your roots be found in the TAO.

Flower from there.

60.

You are not here to harm.

In using the TAO as a template you will see
nonviolence.

There is no violence in the TAO.

Only movement.

So harm no one.

Show by example how to flow in your TAO.

It is total peace.

Flowing.

In the TAO there is only movement of energy from
one form to another.

61.

A great country is like water, it flows.

The TAO is the ocean it flows to, always finding it place there.

This country flowing in the TAO is humble, not being offended easily.

Conflict is avoided.

A great leader understands those who find fault are teaching.

She admits her mistakes and makes changes.

A master knows there is good and bad in everyone, including himself.

A country flowing in the TAO takes care of itself and does not force it's ways on others.

Light are the actions of a country flowing in the TAO.

<u>62.</u>

At the center of all is the TAO.
The center of a good woman.
The center of a bad man.

People now seek honor, the TAO is beyond.
Some seek favor, beyond that too, the TAO.
Bad or good, beyond the TAO.

Leaders should be offered the TAO.
Not help with money or skills.
The TAO will even all things.

The masters enjoy the TAO because there is no
judgment there.
If you want something you find it, in the TAO.
Mistakes do not exist in the TAO.
Love is there.

63.

How can you act without doing?

Use your mind.

Imagine big things as small, at some level they are.

Ponder many as few.

In doing so you can overcome fear and difficulty.

When you judge events then you see them as either easy or difficult.

Do not judge events.

Flow in your TAO allowing events to pass through you.

Then you will clearly see any task is achieved through small steps, in its own order.

A master does not become uptight when doing any task.

Her calm ease of effort never leaves her.

A master does not grasp after greatness, instead allowing it to happen naturally.

Being viewed as great is only the opinion of others, which is a human illusion.

64.

It is easy to feed a tree because it has roots.

A child is easy to correct because they just arrived, trying to learn.

Seashells are easy to break because they are brittle.

Sand is easy to scatter because it is tiny.

It is natural for you to seek order.

Place things in order before trouble arises.

A tiny seed grows a whole forest.

Skyscrapers begin with one brick.

An endless journey begins with your own feet.

Hastiness causes failure.

Trying to force things only makes life more worrisome.

A master takes actions according to the natural flow of things.

He is calm from the beginning until the end.

Not clinging to an outcome.

A master does not try to gain and in doing so she receives all.

He does not interfere in the natural flow of life.

Getting back to basic thinking is her way.

Always reminding friends who they are.

He takes care understanding the TAO and in doing so he cares for all things.

65.

The Masters of the past did not use the TAO to enlighten.

Instead they used it to point the simple way.

People who think they are cleverly smart are hard to govern.

They claim to know all the answers before the question is even finished.

Avoid smart asses, they attract trouble.

A great leader of people is not a smart ass.

A wise leader listens to council, then weighs the best options.

This is called the Mystic Virtue.

Go back to the basic things, the source.

Harmony returns when you relax in your TAO Flow.

<u>66.</u>

Why is the ocean mightier than 1000 streams?

It takes the lowest position, so all streams flow to it naturally.

Therefore it is mightier.

This is why a leader that is loved puts themselves below the people, as a servant.

Listen to how they speak; when they lead they are supporting the people.

A true leader's words and actions help the people move forward.

This is why they look to the TAO.

They strive against no one.

67.

Everyone says my TAO is great, like nothing.

If it were like anything on earth, from the start it would be small.

I have three treasures that I keep on my travels.

First, gentleness.

Second, simplicity.

Third, deciding not to be first.

Because I am gentle, I have courage.

Because I am simple, I can give freely.

Because I am not first, I lead.

Without these three treasures I am worth less than nothing.

<u>68.</u>

A smart warrior does not rush ahead of the line.

Anger is far from him.

Revenge is useless.

An honorable leader does not act superior.

Not competing.

There is a place for the abilities of others.

The TAO is in everything, since before time.

69.

The Master Warrior says this:

I dare not be the aggressor but prefer to be the defender.

I dare not advance an inch but prefer to retreat a yard.

Marching without moving,

without baring an arm,

capturing a foe without a battle,

arming yourself with no weapons.

There is no disaster greater than attacking and finding you underestimated your enemy.

It will cost you your treasure.

Thus it is that when opposing forces meet,

victory goes to those who are flexible, who take no pleasure in the battle.

70.

My writings are easy to understand and easy to
practice.

But no one seems to understand them.

My words have a maker. My steps have a system.

People do not understand this.

So they do not understand me.

Look inside and you will see me written there

A Master wears simple clothes.

And underneath carries jade inside her heart.

71.

It is healthy to know that you do not know.

To think you know when you do not is sick-
mindedness.

When you are sick of being sick you will no longer be
sick.

Masters are not sick because they are sick of sickness;

this is a way to health.

72.

When the people lack a sense of reverence, respect,
dread, and wonder inspired by authority;

disaster will descend upon them.

Give the people plenty of living space.

Let them work without hassle.

Do not micro-manage them, and they will not become
weary of you.

A Master knows herself

but makes no show of herself.

A Master knows his value

but does not exalt himself.

They prefer the natural flow of the TAO to force.

73.

If your courage lies in daring, you will tend to enjoy
killing.

If your courage lies in not daring you will spare
another's life.

Of these two ways, both can be beneficial or harmful.

Heaven dislikes some ways.

Why?

Even a Master has difficulty with such questions.

The TAO is effortless, yet it conquers.

The TAO doesn't speak and yet you respond.

The TAO doesn't summon, yet it attracts.

The TAO is at ease, yet it has no apparent plan.

The TAO's net extends over the whole universe.

Though its net is colossal, nothing has ever slipped
through.

74.

When someone is not afraid of death, isn't it useless to threaten them with death?

If someone was afraid of death and if they would always be arrested and put to death, then who would do wrong?

There is a Lord of Execution whose duty it is to kill.

If you try to fill that function it is like trying to carve wood in place of a master carpenter.

Most likely you will cut your own hands.

75.

Why are the people hungry?

It is because their leaders eat up too much of the tax-grain; that is why the people are hungry.

Why are the people unruly, difficult to govern?

It is due to their leader's interference;

that is why the people are unruly, difficult to govern.

Why do people treat death lightly?

Because their leaders are so grossly absorbed in living; that is why people treat death lightly.

It is wiser to ignore life altogether, than to place too great a value on it.

76.

At birth we are supple and soft.

At death we are stiff and hard.

Grass and trees are flexible and tender when living, but
they are dry and break when dead.

The stiff and hard are helpers of death,

the flexible and soft are helpers of life.

The headstrong army, the hard weapon will be broken.

A mighty tree, invites an axe.

The hard and mighty belong below.

Flexible and soft belong above.

77.

The TAO of heaven is like the bending of a bow.

The high-end is pulled down and the bottom-end is raised up.

The extra length is shortened and the deficient width is expanded.

It is the way of heaven to take where there is too much and to give where there is not enough.

The way of people is opposite.

They take from those who do not have enough in order to give to those who already have too much.

Who will take from their own excesses?

And give to those who need?

Only those who hold to the TAO in their heart.

The Master benefits yet expects no reward, does her work and moves on.

She has no desire to be considered better than others.

78.

Nothing in the universe is softer or more yielding than water.

Water has no equal for attacking

the hard.

None is superior.

Did you know yielding overcomes the rigid? Soft overcomes hard?

The funny thing is, no one applies this knowledge.

Therefore, a Master says:

A person, who has accepted the maliciously false statements and slander, is a leader worthy to offer sacrifice at the country's shrines of earth and grain.

A person, who takes his country's tribulations, is worthy to be a leader among those who dwell there.

Straight seems crooked.

79.

Don't be a fool twice.

After a truce is made between two enemies, some
hatred is bound to remain.

Can this be beneficial?

A Master fulfills the obligations of the agreement and
makes no claim upon others.

A person who has Virtue shares with others.

A person who is vicious takes from others.

The TAO is impartial, constantly offering goodness to
all.

80.

Imagine a small country with very few people.

Even though they could have machines that would increase crops ten to a hundred times, they are not used.

The people really value their lives and have ways to travel, but do not travel very far.

They have boats and carriages but no one uses them much.

They have armor and weapons, with no reason to display them.

These happy people give to writing
and return to the weaving of cords.
They are satisfied with their food.
They have simple pleasing clothes.
Families are safe and happy in their homes.
A happy country this is, with simple ways.

Neighboring countries overlook one another and can
even hear dogs barking and cocks crowing in it.
Even still the people grow old and die
without ever having conflict.

81.

Sincere words are seldom elegant; elegant words are seldom sincere.

Good people do not argue.

The person who argues is seen as bad.

Often the wise do not have great schooling.

Often those with great schooling are not wise.

A Master does not accumulate just to accumulate.

He lives for people. The more he does for others, the more he has and the more he gives to others, the greater his abundance.

The TAO blesses and does not harm.

A Master helps without competing.

TAO TE CHING

Enjoy Stan Atamanchuk's Web site:
http://www.FunToWatch.TV
~~~~~~~
Stan's email address is: cosmicmagnet@yahoo.com
~~~~~~~